W9-CYY-529

HUNTING: PURSUING WILD GAME!™

AVOIDING DANGER ON THE HUNT

PHILIP WOLNY

rosen publishing's
rosen central®

New York

Published in 2013 by The Rosen Publishing Group, Inc.
29 East 21st Street, New York, NY 10010

First Edition

Library of Congress Cataloging-in-Publication Data

Wolny, Philip.
Avoiding danger on the hunt/Philip Wolny.
    p. cm.—(Hunting—pursuing wild game!)
Includes bibliographical references and index.
ISBN 978-1-4488-8278-6 (library binding)—
ISBN 978-1-4488-8283-0 (pbk.)—
ISBN 978-1-4488-8284-7 (6-pack)
1. Hunting—Safety measures—Juvenile literature. 2. Firearms—Safety measures—
Juvenile literature. I. Title.
SK39.5.W65 2013
639'.10289—dc23
                                                                                    2012022069

Manufactured in the United States of America

CPSIA Compliance Information: Batch #W13YA: For further information, contact Rosen Publishing, New York, New York, at 1-800-237-9932.

CONTENTS

A father and his teenaged daughter step carefully through the quiet woods. They have been hunting turkey for a couple of hours, with no luck so far. But they are in high spirits, excited to harvest a "gobbler." They enter a thick patch of woods, using their turkey calls.

In a heartbeat, their luck seems to change: they hear some rustling in the dense trees, about 30 yards (27 meters) ahead. The daughter lifts her gun into shooting position, excited by the sudden movement she sees down the barrel of her shotgun. She is so lost in the moment that it takes her a couple of seconds to hear her father firmly telling her to stand down. Filled with adrenalin, yet confused, she obeys his stern order, putting her shotgun back into a "field carry." A human voice calls out from beyond the trees. Another hunter steps into view.

Her father breathes a big sigh of relief. Everyone involved is lucky to be fine, but this scenario could have ended very differently—in injury, and even death. The father reminds his daughter about one important rule: never aim at anything while hunting unless you are sure it is game.

Every year, many hunters—and sometimes innocent bystanders—are hurt or killed while attempting to

Hunters afield stand holding their firearms in a safe carry, wearing proper hunter orange.

harvest wild game. Whether in deep wilderness or in more controlled hunting preserves, there are many dangers to look out for. The things that can wrong are not limited to irresponsible use of firearms, either.

Hunter injuries and fatalities occur in many ways, both anticipated and completely unexpected. Holding or firing a rifle or shotgun improperly might put a bullet or shot into a hunting companion or even a non-hunter far away. Guns and ammunition can suffer from defects or malfunction. Other equipment used during a hunt, such as damaged boats or faulty tree stands, might fail or cause injury.

As in the scenario above, the thrill of the chase can often cause younger or inexperienced hunters to forget important safety rules. A very wise and experienced hunter once said, "You can really get caught up in the hunt and make rash decisions that put you or others in danger. If you have to think twice about how safe something is while on the chase, it is probably a bad idea." Numerous fatalities and injuries occur yearly when hunters drop their firearms or carry them thoughtlessly. Inexperienced or careless hunters can lose their way, suffer needlessly from hypothermia, or injure themselves by tripping while walking or running through rough terrain. Getting too little sleep or nourishment, or consuming alcohol or narcotics (legal or otherwise) can be fatal mistakes. Depending on the game, knowing how to deal with wildlife, especially large animals, can also make the difference between safe hunting and a dangerous situation. Wild predators, and even animals that have been brought down, can injure or kill careless hunters.

With all of these dangers to consider, hunters must also select the proper gear and use it responsibly, secure the correct training and permits for their state and the type of game they are harvesting, learn how to handle emergencies, and much more.

However extensive all of these measures sound, they are well worth it. Despite the statistics, millions of people worldwide hunt responsibly every year. It is imperative to learn all of the tips, techniques, and strategies for avoiding danger on the hunt and staying safe and healthy. This will help ensure a long life full of wonderful experiences shared with friends and family members out in the field and wilderness.

CHAPTER I

BEFORE HEADING OUT

Avoiding danger on the hunt starts long before going into the field. Preparing ahead of time includes many different aspects of hunting, including safety training, learning the proper use and care of weapons and equipment, and getting acquainted with the wilderness. One important thing to remember is "an ounce of prevention is worth a pound of cure."

Proper Licensing

Each state establishes its own rules for hunting and hunting safety. Some states require junior hunting licenses for any-one under a certain age—say, below the age of sixteen. In many states, everyone must first take a hunter education course. Other states allow youngsters to accompany others on a hunt without a license, but they must be with someone with a valid hunting

An instructor hands a .22 round to sixth-grader Ramsey Schumacher at the Juneau Hunter Education Shooting Complex in Juneau, Alaska.

license who is of a certain age. While some areas mandate hunter education for all types of game, others do not for small game or for hunting animals considered "vermin," such as squirrels.

Even in the rare case that it is optional, it is important that everyone take a safety course, especially if they have little firearm or hunting experience. Gaining knowledge from trained professionals can only add to the wisdom gained from family members or relatives.

Also, most courses offered must meet certain minimum standards of the International Hunting Education Association (IHEA). It is likely that taking a course in one's home state will give a hunter the right to register for a hunting license in nearly every part of North America.

Hunter Education

Hunter education courses typically include a combination of classroom teaching, homework, and field instruction. Most courses last at least ten hours. Courses in Tennessee, for example, last from twelve to sixteen hours.

A major component of any course is firearms and bowhunting education and instruction. Students learn about modern firearms and ammunition, how to handle and store guns, and marksmanship (how to shoot and use bows). This includes the history of firearms and archery. The Ten Commandments of Firearms Safety are also vital. Firearms training

Instructor Glen Waggoner *(second from right)* instructs online hunter education course students in proper walking form during a field day in McPherson County, Kansas.

usually includes mandatory live-fire exercises. Hunter education also covers hunting ethics, including respect for wildlife, the environment, private and public property, fellow hunters, and the general public. It stresses sportsmanship and covers topics like wildlife management and identification and the proper handling of harvested game.

Of course, safety is a major part of the curriculum, above and beyond the use of firearms and bows themselves. Courses cover basic rules and tips for survival in the wilderness, how to avoid hypothermia, and how to deal with emergencies and administer first aid in case of injury. Finally, hunter education includes how to prepare for the hunt, laws and regulations, and important outdoor equipment and gear needed to stay safe and hunt responsibly and effectively.

The usual requirement to pass the course and thus obtain a hunter education certificate is to pass a multiple-choice test. Also, while not every state has a minimum age cutoff for students, it is not recommended for younger children (under the age of nine or so) because it may be too difficult for them.

Gearing Up

Just as hunters ready their minds (and bodies) for the hunt, they must consider the various equipment and gear needed for a productive and safe hunt, including choice of firearms. Among the most important bits of advice any seasoned hunter will tell you is the old scouting motto: "Be Prepared!"

Maintaining Gear

Maintaining and inspecting any necessary gear or equipment should be done well in advance of a trip afield. Waiting until the night before

A waterfowler in camouflage retrieves a harvested duck. Waterfowling is one of the types of hunting that does not require the wearing of hunter orange.

is a mistake; there is always the chance of overlooking something at the last minute. Though it might seem like a lot to cover, it is better to find out now if something important needs to be repaired or replaced, rather than suffer when already afield and it is too late for any necessary fixes.

All clothing and equipment should be checked to make sure it is not damaged or deteriorated, especially from previous hunting seasons, and that it works as it should. Check boots and other protective gear for cracks or dry rot. A waterfowler, for example, should inspect the waders that will be needed in wetland areas. Cleaning gear of all mud, dirt, and debris goes a long way in preventing it from falling apart or failing during a hunt and preserves it for future seasons.

With newly purchased gear, it is important that one carefully reviews instructions and researches its proper use and maintenance. Every piece of equipment should be opened and inspected, and all its pieces accounted for. A tent might be missing stakes, poles, or other parts, for instance. Whether it is a pair of boots that suddenly takes on water or shooting glasses that turn out to be broken and unusable, the last thing a hunter wants is to abandon the hunt or try to work around faulty or damaged equipment. Doing so could compromise his or her safety (or fellow hunters').

Dress Smart

Every year, many hunters still go afield hopelessly unprepared. Dress for the weather and terrain. This is especially true if hunting overnight for a few days. Temperatures and weather can rise and fall dramatically, despite what the weather forecast predicts, and rain and snow can hit unexpectedly.

Hunters pursuing nearly any type of game (except for turkeys and migratory birds), must wear hunter orange afield (also called blaze

Make Your Location Known

Whenever hunting with others, everyone must make it known where they are at all times. News media reported in February 2006 that the then-vice president of the United States, Dick Cheney, had accidentally shot a fellow hunting companion, seventy-eight-year-old attorney Harry Whittington, during a quail hunt on a private hunting preserve. Cheney admitted having just one beer hours earlier. But the other hunters agreed that Whittington was largely to blame because he had not announced his location to his companions. Whittington suffered birdshot injuries to his face, neck, and chest but recovered.

orange), unless they are in a tree stand at least 12 feet (3.7 meters) off the ground. Exact rules vary, but this means hunters must wear a jacket, vest, or at the very least a full-size hunting hat or cap. Deer and many other species cannot detect this type of orange in the wild, while humans can easily see it. Camouflage is no substitute.

First-Aid Kit

A good first-aid kit runs about $50 or $60 and contains supplies and medication for minor or major wounds. It should contain a combination of Band-Aids, bandages, gauze, wound dressings, medical tape, and scissors for treating minor wounds (and preventing major ones from worsening). Medications usually include aspirin, ibuprofen, a diamode (diarrhea medication), an antihistamine (for allergies and insect stings), an antibiotic ointment/cream, and iodine (a water purifier

A standard wilderness survival kit contains basic items that hunters require for safety and emergency first aid afield.

and disinfectant). Hunters can and should add extra items, depending on region, weather, and type of game.

If any member of the party is allergic to bee, wasp, or hornet stings, a first-aid tool known as an epinephrine auto-injector is a must. Allergic reactions can include swelling that can stop a victim's breathing. A dose of epinephrine temporarily relieves this, giving the victim time to seek emergency care. Without it, a sting far out in the wilderness could easily be fatal.

Also, all members of a hunting party should double-check that they pack any necessary medication or items that they may need, whether out for the day or for overnight hunting expeditions. The last thing anyone needs is to realize mid-hunt that they have forgotten their asthma or diabetes medication. Hunters must remember to take their proper dosage of medications while afield.

Survival Kit

In addition, there are some basic items that help hunters navigate the wilderness and are crucial in case of an emergency, like getting lost or being stuck overnight. These are often part of any store-bought survival kit. Such a kit may include a flashlight, compass, hunting knife and/or multitool (a combination of knives and useful tools), fire flint and tinders, wind- and waterproof matches and strikers, nylon cord, high-SPF sunblock, and signal mirrors and/or flares (useful for getting the attention of park rangers or other faraway rescue personnel). It should also include a thermal or solar blanket (for warmth), a wire blade survival saw, a small "survival" shovel, emergency food and water supplies, and extra batteries.

Survival kits will usually also include the first-aid items listed earlier. One should carefully consider what is really necessary for a few hours afield versus what is required for a long weekend of hunting and camping out. There is a big difference between what you can load up a car or truck with if you plan to hunt close to your vehicle and what you can carry safely and comfortably while backpacking farther afield.

Where to Hunt

Long before embarking, hunters need a plan. Where the hunt happens is important. Staying safe goes hand-in-hand with avoiding

U.S.
RESERVATION
BOUNDARY
MARK
DO NOT
DISTURB

PUBLIC
HUNTING

A bowhunter carrying a harvested wild turkey walks past a sign allowing public hunting in the area.

danger—from the law, that is. Hunters must make sure that it is legal to harvest game in a particular area. In some regions, this includes getting permission ahead of time from property owners and avoiding hunting in posted areas—that is, property that is clearly marked "no hunting" or "no trespassing."

Getting Permission

In most states, hunters must receive written or verbal permission to hunt from property owners. In other states—for instance, New Hampshire—the public have greater rights to hunt on private land if it is not posted. Other states allow hunting only where signs explicitly say so. However, hunters should always seek permission out of respect and common courtesy. Also, a landowner will likely know if there are dangerous conditions that hunters should know about before entering the property.

Many states have rules barring hunting within a certain distance of a home, farm, or business; in New Hampshire, for instance, it is 300 feet (91 meters). Hunting laws vary widely among states; regulations may change from one season to the next. Check online or consult a game warden or wildlife official to make sure. In many states, special hunting permits might be required well ahead of the season and can often be limited, distributed only on a "first-come, first-served" basis. This is often true for controlled hunting of specific species. Also, be aware that some owners charge money for the privilege of hunting on their property.

Never Assume...

Even if you have permission to hunt on particular land (public or private), never assume that you are alone in a particular area. Not everyone abides by the law, and there is always the chance that you may encounter poachers. Assuming otherwise is unsafe; members of your party might let their guard down and end up hurting someone else or suffering injury from the irresponsible actions of strangers.

Finally, make sure that everyone has obtained all the necessary licenses and permits necessary for your state, type of game, and season you are hunting in. Waterfowlers, for example, need to obtain both state and federal "duck stamps." States have different rules and times for bowhunting, too. Just as you should do a gear check early on, research on these details should be done well before hunting.

Knowing Where to Go

Surprisingly, many people neglect one of the most important steps: obtaining a map of the hunting area. The United States Geological Survey has thousands of maps available online, as well as at its many branch offices nationwide. A state's fish and game department is a good place to look, too, as are local county archives. Carefully reviewing a map can also help hunters plan on prime locations for game (for example, near water sources like streams and rivers).

Before leaving, hunters should always let someone at home know their destination, who is going, how long they will be away, and when exactly they plan to return. They should also figure out a contingency plan—what the folks at home should do if they do not return when expected.

CHAPTER 2

WEAPON SAFETY

It is all too easy to forget that hunting is not a game but a deadly serious activity. Firearms and bows are designed for killing. Everyone who hunts, whether novices going afield or seasoned veterans, must keep safety the most important priority, even above harvesting game.

There are some vital rules that all hunters should internalize early on. Known informally as the Ten Commandments of Firearm Safety, their focus is on preventing injury and death. Several versions of this list exist on the Internet. Most of them include the following basics.

1. Keep All Firearms Pointed in a Safe Direction

Perhaps the most important rule is to always keep the muzzle of a firearm pointed in a

A hunter hands a firearm to his companion, properly aiming the muzzle into the air to ensure maximum safety for both of them.

safe direction—in other words, any direction that will not cause injury or death to a person if the gun accidentally discharges. Until a hunter is 100 percent ready to shoot, he or she must keep fingers off the trigger and keep the gun's safety on.

2. Keep Guns Unloaded When Not in Use

A gun should be loaded with ammunition only while a hunter is in the field and in active pursuit of game. Never keep loaded guns at home, even under lock and key. Do not drive to and from the field with loaded

A hunter loads a rifle. Proper techniques for handling ammo and firearms are among the first things to learn before going afield.

weapons, even stashed in a trunk or the back of a truck. No matter how well someone secures a loaded gun, there is always a chance it will go off. Imagine a rifle firing through the trunk of a car and hitting a passenger or a fellow motorist.

A hunter passing a gun to another hunter should always check the gun thoroughly to make sure it is unloaded. Always carefully unload your weapon before putting it away in a car or at camp. Both the chamber and magazine should be free of ammo.

It is also a bad idea to put down a loaded firearm, no matter how safe the situation seems. Texas waterfowler Perry Price learned the hard way in January 2008, according to the Associated Press. Price had just bagged a goose and was about to release his excited hunting dog from the cab of his truck. In a freak occurrence, as he lay the gun down inside the cab, Price's Labrador accidentally released the trigger of his shotgun while jumping around. The gun discharged through the tailgate and into Price's thigh. Sadly, Price lost too much blood from a severed artery and died soon after. Such tragedies occur more often than we imagine.

Hunters should always unload their weapons when negotiating difficult terrain or tackling any obstacle where they might lose control of their firearm and thus accidentally discharge it. This includes climbing trees or getting into tree stands or blinds, negotiating fences or ladders, or jumping across ditches. Putting down or leaning a loaded gun while doing another activity leaves open the possibility that the gun could fall and unexpectedly discharge.

3. Never Rely Solely on a Gun's Safety

While the safety should always be on, it is also dangerous to get overconfident about the safety. A gun is a mechanical device, and it cannot be assumed that it will always work properly, no matter how well made or new it is. Human error tends to cause more accidents than mechanical failure.

Always keep the safety on when not about to fire, but always act as if the safety is off. You may think the safety is on, when it is not. Even the best, most experienced hunters sometimes forget, especially in the heat of the moment. The safety may have disengaged without the handler's knowledge.

4. Be Sure of Your Target, and What's Beyond It

Hunters need to be 100 percent sure that a sighted target is indeed game and not another person, pet, or livestock. Even experienced hunters cannot always positively tell what movement in brush or thick forest actually is. Never fire on a hunch.

Hunters also need to be extremely careful about what lies beyond a target. A poorly aimed shot can travel far off into the wilderness and injure others. Rocks and other natural objects, like trees, can cause ammunition to ricochet, or bounce off, in unexpected directions. Even bodies of water like lakes or streams can cause ricochets. Every shooter should make sure that there is a safe backstop behind any targeted game. Firing at a target without a backstop, especially if a hunter increases the angle from zero degrees (even just slightly), can result in shots traveling thousands of yards away. A shot can also pass right through a target.

Firing without absolutely positive identification leads to numerous deaths and injuries annually. In January 2012, the *Boston Globe* reported on how off-duty Massachusetts state trooper John Bergeron accidentally wounded a Norton, MA, resident, sixty-six-year-old Cheryl

Blair, while hunting deer. Bergeron aimed and fired at what he thought was a deer. In reality, it was the tail of one of Blair's golden retriever dogs. Lucky to be alive, Blair suffered a leg wound that left her limping with a cane and experiencing constant pain. Even a trained policeman and longtime hunter like Bergeron can make a tragic mistake.

5. Use the Right Ammunition

Hunters must use the right ammunition for their firearms and consult their gun owner's manuals to determine what that is. Double-check any shells or other ammo purchased to make sure it is all the same. Ammunition cartridges and shells are stamped with the gauge, while the caliber and gauge of a firearm are usually displayed on a gun's barrel.

One all-too-common mistake is using a 20-gauge shell in the chamber of a 12-gauge shotgun. The 20-gauge will typically not go through the barrel, and the gun will misfire. However, the chamber will appear to be empty, making it easy to make the potentially fatal mistake of loading a 12-gauge shell behind it. Firing a second shot slams the second shell into the 20-gauge shell. The gun may explode in one's hands; this is called a "12-20" burst.

6. If a Gun Fails to Fire When Pulling the Trigger, Beware

A gun that fails to fire demands great caution. If this happens, the hunter must remember rule one: point the muzzle in a safe direction, put the safety on, open the action, and carefully unload the gun and discard the cartridge. Always assume that the gun could discharge at any time, and keep your face away from the breech.

Two hunters are skeet shooting with proper eye and ear protection, an absolute must for both competitive shooting and hunting.

7. Always Protect Eyes and Ears When Shooting

When hunting (or range shooting), protecting eyes and ears is a must. Falling shot residue, cartridge casings, and other foreign objects, including twigs and branches, can irritate or damage your eyes. Protective eyewear should be shatter-proof. Remember that a gun malfunctioning can easily blind a hunter.

Guns are loud, and ear protection is vital; in the field, this usually means wearing earplugs. Failing to do so could result in permanent hearing loss or damage over the years. This is a common health problem for hunters who do not take ear protection seriously.

8. Ensure That Gun Barrels Are Free of Obstructions

Check the chamber and magazine by opening the action every time to make sure there is no ammunition inside before loading. A gun can bulge or burst from extra pressure even from small amounts of debris obstructing the barrel. Snow, mud, and lubricant are all potential hazards. It may seem obvious, but never, ever try to rid the barrel of obstructions by shooting.

Also, hunters that drop weapons need to take apart their guns and check for obstructions. Foreign matter can enter the barrel undetected. Pay careful attention to how a weapon sounds or behaves. A weak or otherwise unusual recoil might signal that a barrel check is necessary.

9. Avoid Altering or Modifying Guns, and Service Them Regularly

Firearms are produced in very specific ways. Avoid modifying a gun on your own, no matter how handy you think you are. Amateurs often lack the proper tools and training. A hunter desiring to do so needs the services of a professional gunsmith. Beginners should always clean and maintain their gun with help from an experienced hunter. Like any machine, guns experience wear and tear and break down. Improper maintenance is another cause of injuries.

Firearms should be properly cleaned and oiled and stored in the off-season. Dirt and moisture can impair functioning. Rust can render a gun useless or dangerous. Consult the owner's manual (or ask a gunsmith) for proper methods and materials to use for cleaning, lubrication, and storage. Double-check to make sure that a rifle or shotgun works—well before a hunt, during the off-season. It is unlikely that a gunsmith can do same-day firearm tune-ups or repairs.

10. Know Your Firearm

Guns vary widely according to the user and type of game. Younger and/or novice hunters might use less powerful rifles or shotguns; otherwise, they may be unable to handle them.

A man lubricates a firearm. Keeping guns well maintained is crucial for their proper and safe functioning.

They must weigh their ability to use a gun versus hunting ethics. It is cruel to harvest game in a way that makes an animal suffer needlessly because the caliber of gun was too weak to efficiently kill it with one shot.

Different guns demand different ways of handling and carrying them. Whether receiving a gun passed down from someone else or taking a new weapon afield, the novice hunter should read and take to heart everything in a gun's manual before use.

Hunt Sober!

Aside from drugs and underage drinking being illegal, it is an absolutely terrible idea to consume any mind-altering substance any time before or during a hunt. Shoot sober at all times. Even one beer well before a hunt can compromise one's thinking ability, aim, and reaction time. Drugs and/or alcohol and firearms are a lethal combination that kills or maims far too many hunters.

Similarly, consult a doctor if you take any prescription medication to make sure that it does not affect your mindset, concentration, or judgment while afield. Never go out hunting if you feel fatigued or in the least bit impaired due to medicine, whether prescription or over-the-counter, like cold medicine. It is a terrible idea to hunt while sick for the same reason.

Hunting with Bows

Many firearm rules also apply to bowhunting. Bowhunters should not point a nocked arrow anywhere it may cause unwanted harm. They should learn about and maintain their weapon and avoid carelessness in the field. Maintain your tackle (bowhunting equipment) regularly, and have it serviced regularly or if things feel "off." Avoid exposing it to extreme temperature changes or humidity, as these affect the gear's condition.

Just as hunters armed with loaded firearms should not attempt difficult maneuvers, bowhunters must observe similar rules. A nocked arrow could release and hit someone else, and sharp arrowheads can seriously gore a bowhunter in the event of a fall or stumble. Keep all

Like firearms, bowhunting equipment requires proper maintenance and extreme care, both during the off-season and while afield.

hunting knives sheathed and secured, too. Bows should be unstrung, and arrows should be carried with a protective cover or in a quiver. Ensuring that arrows do not work their way through a quiver prevents scratching or goring; always inspect quivers for damage.

There is no excuse for shooting at game without being sure of the target. This is perhaps even more true in bowhunting because arrows travel over shorter ranges and because an ethical and effective kill shot can usually only be made by positively sighting game. A bowhunter arguably has a higher standard of identification.

CHAPTER 3

AVOIDING DANGER AFIELD

The wilderness is an incredible resource— a beautiful place to relax and unwind—but it demands respect and reverence. The natural world is filled with unexpected dangers. Much like their firearms or bows, hunters must treat this wild environment (and its creatures) with caution.

Braving the Elements

Among the most important natural factors is weather. Hunters afield are at the mercy of the elements. The weather can greatly aid a hunt: ideal conditions can help hunters strategize on pursuing game. It can also be a great nuisance—and a deadly threat.

A man and his black Labrador puppy hunt ptarmigan in Granite Basin near Juneau, Alaska, during winter. Extreme weather demands extreme care.

The Cold

Depending on the region and game season, hunters may face extreme cold, especially early in the morning or toward the end of a hunt. Icy conditions can make it extra dangerous to negotiate an unfamiliar wilderness, especially in steep terrain. One wrong slip can mean a twisted ankle, a broken limb, or even death. Unprotected hands or other extremities can lead to frostbite. The cold can numb a hunter's hands and make it difficult to handle guns and gear. Some warmer gloves might be too thick for proper firearm handling.

Guns can also behave differently in extreme cold. Lubricants might "gel up" and cause potentially dangerous misfires. Double-check your gun for snow or ice building up and obstructing the bore.

On Thin Ice

Other hunters invite danger by crossing frozen bodies of water, especially large ones, like lakes. They risk perishing in icy water below. Unstable ice can crack further, endangering rescuers. Hunters wearing many layers or weighted down with equipment are in greater danger of drowning.

"Cotton Kills"

Many hunters, hikers, and other outdoors enthusiasts repeat a famous motto: "cotton kills." Wearing cotton clothes is bad in cooler weather. Cotton transfers moisture from sweat to the material itself. This eliminates its insulating properties and quickly steals heat from the body. Even small amounts of moisture in a cool environment can cause problems on the hunt.

As an alternative, hunters should wear non-cotton materials such as clothes made of polypropylene, wool, or polyester, in layers. Polyester and polypropylene are particularly good choices because they are hydrophobic. This means that they tend to transfer moisture away from the material closest to the skin, keeping the wearer warm and dry.

Avoid the dangers of hypothermia, a drop in human body temperature below 95 degrees Fahrenheit (35 degrees Celsius). From being underdressed, to not having the proper gear while wading through water, to capsizing a boat, there are many ways to harm oneself while hunting in cold weather. Prolonged exposure to the cold can cause confusion, brain damage, and even death.

The Heat

Heat can also be dangerous. Even in moderate weather, remember to bring water and properly hydrate. If you run out of water, it is recommended that you purify water from the wild using iodine or other

A man takes a sip of water on the hunt. Keep properly hydrated at all times, especially in hot weather.

methods. As in cold weather, wearing cotton as the innermost layer during a warm-weather hunt is a bad idea because it increases body heat.

Heat exhaustion affects reaction times and judgment, increasing the chance of making dangerous errors. If it gets worse, it can turn into heat stroke, a dangerous physical state that brings on dangerous hallucinations and can lead to seizures, heart attacks, coma, and death. Any hunter experiencing even minor symptoms should be cooled down, brought into a shady area, and taken for emergency medical care as soon as possible.

Which Way to Go?

Hunters sometimes get lost. In a worst-case scenario, they might use the sun's position in the sky to get oriented. However, cloud cover, thickly forested wilderness, and other factors might cancel out the sun's usefulness. Skilled woodsmen, survivalists, and scouts may have specialized knowledge on how to navigate due to natural clues.

One can easily prevent getting lost. Obtain and study maps of the hunting area ahead of time. Driving out to the area a week before to explore is also an option. Make copies of the map, circle key positions, and leave one copy at home and

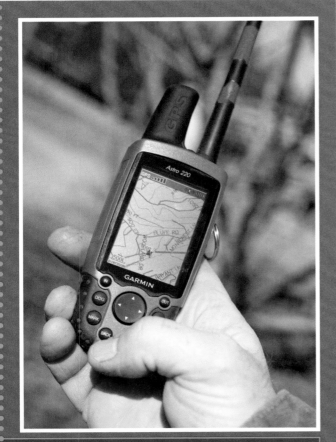

Tennessee hunter Shannon Robinson holds a GPS device that tracks his coon-hunting dogs.

one in your vehicle. If you miss your estimated time of arrival, others will have a good idea of your location.

Another common-sense item to bring is a compass (remember: learn how to use it). At least one hunting companion should have a fully charged cellphone on vibrate; remember to check the signal near the hunting area beforehand. While you should confirm the rules of their use with your local department of natural resources or park service, two-way radios are also a handy emergency measure. A device that uses the Global Positioning System (GPS) is also a great tool; many phones also have built-in GPS of some kind.

Finding the way back to camp or a vehicle will prevent you from spending an uncomfortable and potentially dangerous night in the woods. Anyone who has ever been caught near dusk still out on the trail or hunt knows how hard it is to navigate the woods at night.

Dangerous Waters

Hunters should take extra care around water and wetland areas. Waterfowlers, for example, often hunt from boats or standing in relatively deep water. Respect the power of water much like you respect guns and the wilderness itself. Even a very low level of rushing water can knock a person down and sweep him or her downstream. One misstep while hunting from a boat can land someone in the water or capsize the boat, endangering everyone. Avoid sudden and abrupt movements while on the water. Carefully inspect the boat before embarking, always wear a lifejacket, and keep gear in watertight containers.

Up in the Air: Tree Stands

Among the most common hunting injuries are mishaps related to tree stands (also known as deer stands), the platforms that hunters use to

A hunter surveys the landscape for white-tailed deer from a tree stand near Platteville, Wisconsin.

survey their environment far better than from the ground. By some accounts, tree-stand accidents make up as much as a third of hunter deaths.

Use a climbing belt to ascend and descend, and always use a safety belt or harness in a tree stand. Never climb up while carrying anything—especially not a firearm, bow, or arrows. You can use a separate rope (a haul line) to carefully hoist items up. Most tree-stand incidents happen while climbing up or down. Inspect both permanent and temporary stands before use, and examine commercial stands for missing or loose nuts and buts. Permanent stands may deteriorate from the elements or from use by others.

When climbing up, patience and stability are key. Never shift all your weight onto a single branch. Keep at least one hand and one foot on a solid, tested branch while inspecting the next hold. Climbing directly onto a stand is not recommended; in some cases, it may be damaged or dislodged. Climb slightly higher, and lower yourself onto it. Boots that will not skid on surfaces are best for climbing.

One danger comes from the long hours some hunters spend in a tree stand: falling asleep. Hunters can injure themselves (even if they are safely strapped in, as they should be) and might even misfire their weapon while asleep. Hunters beginning to feel drowsy should stretch and move around as much as possible to wake up. Drowsiness can compromise a hunter's ability to think clearly.

Dangerous Game and Wild Animals

Some hunters choose to pursue inherently dangerous game, such as bears or wild boars. Most animals shy away from humans when possible. It is often true that they're more afraid of you than you are of them. But many creatures can become extremely aggressive if threatened or if their young are in danger. Even smaller specimens of bear are far stronger and faster than humans and can easily kill hunters that provoke them. Wild boars, hunted throughout North America, can be very belligerent, and their large size and tusks make for a deadly combination. Remaining alert and cautious at all times is the hunter's first defense against an unexpected run-in with a dangerous creature.

Another dangerous game animal that has become more popular among hunters recently is the bison. Once nearly extinct, it is now mainly hunted on private land in the western United States. These quick, very large animals can easily charge a hunter and pound him or her into the ground. In certain areas, bison are considered more dangerous than bears.

Hunters should educate themselves not only on the type of game they will be hunting, but also about any other animals they may encounter. Familiarize yourself with their habits. Learn the emergency steps you may need to take if you stumble too closely upon a bear or other wild predator.

Fight or Flight?

It is a nightmare scenario for many hunters: accidentally running into a deadly predator. While far more deaths result from firearm and tree-stand accidents, there is always a chance, however small, that you may need to make a crucial decision one day between standing your ground versus running away.

Unfortunately, there is no fail-safe rule for dealing with any particular species of animal. Just as people have very different personalities, animals will not always act predictably. Some mountain lions are more aggressive than others. The same is true for bears, bison, wild boars, and many other species.

One "rule" that many hunters share regarding bears, big cats, and other predators is that it is often a mistake to run or show weakness or fear, especially if a predator is very close to you. Bears and big cats can run faster than humans. If all else fails, stand your ground, make a great deal of noise, and attempt to look bigger than you really are. For instance—take off a layer of clothing and lift it up over your head. This fools some animals into thinking you are much bigger than you are in

A bear is sighted by a photographer in the bushes. Hunters must know how to deal with and prevent injury and death when encountering wild predators.

reality and scares them off. These measures, however, are useless if a bear or other large animal is menacing you.

Novice hunters should consult their more experienced mentors and companions on how to properly react to such dangerous encounters. Again, in many cases, there is no exactly right or wrong approach.

Bear Repellent

In December 2008, *Field & Stream* reported how Mark Matheny and his hunting companion were bowhunting in Montana in 1992 when they stumbled upon a grizzly bear sow (female) nursing two cubs. Charged by the grizzly, they were both attacked. The men suffered serious wounds and would have probably perished if not for Matheny's partner shooting pepper spray at the bear, which eventually ran away.

This near-death experience influenced Matheny to switch careers and start his own company selling "bear spray," a stronger version of pepper spray (generally marketed for self-defense against humans). The magazine also reported that a Brigham Young University study of human/bear encounters over a twenty-year period showed that, in cases in which pepper spray was used, bears were halted or ran off 92 percent of the time.

If a hunter is lucky, some nonviolent methods of avoiding contact with, for example, bears, might work before weapons are needed. A hunter sighting a bear from far enough away can attempt to circle the bear and go upwind of it. Human scent often discourages a bear's approach. Hunters should also attempt to gain the high ground over a bear and place obstacles in its way. One should never turn one's back on a bear; instead, back away slowly. Dropping gear like a backpack or other items on the way may also distract it. Climb a tree if at all possible, and avoid eye contact.

Obviously, one's firearm is a crucial line of defense. But a charging predator may not be stopped immediately by the initial shot, especially if a hunter panics or aims poorly. At times, it might actually provoke an attack.

CHAPTER 4

ETHICS, SPORTSMANSHIP, AND SAFETY

Good sportsmanship, ethics, and following the rules go hand-in-hand with hunting safety. As a hunter gains experience, he or she realizes that, rather than limiting the freedom and adventure that hunting offers, rules and regulations allow for millions to enjoy the sport and pass it on to future generations. Exploring some of the written (and unwritten) rules can help novices appreciate the power and responsibility of this sport.

Hunting: Right and Wrong

There is much debate within the hunting community about how hunters should hunt. Legal hunting includes whatever the state and/or federal law permits for a particular area and species. It covers what kinds of game can be harvested, how much, and the particular means to do so. This may include the caliber of weapons that are allowed for any particular game. Certain weapons may be considered too extreme, while others are not powerful enough to bring down game without considerable pain and suffering.

Fair Chase

Fair-chase hunting is a set of rules, often unofficial, among hunters that guide how to harvest game in an ethical and/or sportsmanlike way. The

An elk hunter harvests his heavy catch with an all-terrain vehicle (ATV) at Crazy French Ranch in Trinidad, Colorado.

main idea behind fair chase is that humans should not have an unfair advantage over animals, including giving the game a fair chance to escape. Fair-chase hunters will not use certain tactics even if they happen to be legal.

For example, while many states allow hunting animals like wolves or wild boars from helicopters, many hunters find this tactic unsporting and inhumane—even repugnant. Some defend the tactic in that it provides the hunter with much greater safety overall than risking coming into close contact with aggressive game. Fair-chase hunters will argue that that is exactly the point: allowing hunters such an unfair advantage is unsporting, not unlike punching a person who is in handcuffs and claiming it is a fair fight.

An Unfair Advantage?

There are other hunting methods that allow for much greater safety for a hunter from potentially dangerous game. Herding or chasing animals from the air is one way. Another is herding or chasing game using motorized vehicles, such as all-terrain vehicles (ATVs). Pretty much all game has a natural fear of the loud noise produced by man-made engines.

Similar hunting methods take advantage of the terrain or hunting area itself. For instance, some hunters take advantage of fencing and other natural barriers to prevent animals the chance of escape.

Baiting and Trapping

Hunters may use traps or drug animals to make it easier (and technically safer) to pick them off. Luring animals with food has also become controversial. Deer baiting—in which food is placed near hunting blinds or stands to lure deer within closer range—is favored by many hunters.

Hunter Chad Stewart lays out corn to bait deer that have become a nuisance in the Cleveland suburb of Solon, Ohio.

Bowhunters especially endorse it because it helps them harvest game with precision and accuracy.

Trapping can be controversial because many consider it both unfair and painfully cruel. It is one thing to use trapping if the desired game animal is one's main food source. However, most hunters do not hunt because they are hungry. While there is debate about how safe traps are, some opponents believe that hikers, hunters, and hunting dogs are endangered by their use.

Harvesting Safely

Humane harvesting of game is not only the right thing to do, it is also important for safety's sake. An effective kill shot eliminates not only the needless suffering of the animal, but also the danger, however small, that the hunter will be hurt or even killed by an injured, frightened creature. A hunt does not end with the kill shot. No one is home free until game is successfully harvested. No matter the size of the kill, nor one's initial assessment that an animal is dead, it is important to confirm that a downed animal presents no danger.

In November 2011, the *Fort Wayne Journal Gazette* reported that the body of sixty-two-year-old hunter Paul J. Smith was discovered at the site where he had killed a buck (male deer). An autopsy, pieced together with a phone call Smith had made earlier to his son, allowed investigators to determine that Smith had struggled with the deer after shooting it from a tree stand. He likely died from the deer kicking him in the abdominal area. As rare as such deaths are, they underscore that hunters must always be extra careful when tagging and field-dressing game.

Obeying the Law

Fair-chase hunters generally stick closely to hunting rules and regulations. This is not to say that others do not, but that playing by the rules is an important part of fair-chase doctrine. Many fair-chase advocates believe that hunting is not merely a sport, but a tradition and way of life that also helps conserve nature, including animal species and our shared national resources. They point out that when animals are not given a fair chance at escape, it is not really hunting but simply murder or killing. Following this philosophy, a true sportsman will take the

A game official speaks with a hunter roadside. Staying within the law both benefits individual hunters and preserves hunting as a lifestyle and tradition.

extra risk in hunting an aggressive predator (within legal bounds) one-on-one, without a host of unfair advantages.

An Unseen Danger: Disease

Danger afield is not limited to accidents, animal attacks, or other similarly obvious pitfalls. Wild animals can carry diseases. Proper inspection and harvesting of kills goes a long way to eliminating most of these dangers. The American Veterinary Medical Association provides many common-sense precautions for avoiding infection from harvested game.

Hunters should avoid handling or eating game exhibiting strange behavior while alive or having unusual body abnormalities that may indicate disease, including strange smells or discharges. Always wear gloves when handling and field-dressing game. Cut away and safely discard wounded tissue. Minimize contact with brain or spinal tissues. Wear safety glasses when removing antlers from any animal. Make sure that intestines and their contents are kept away from meat. Wash hands thoroughly with soap and water or alcohol-based cleansers and wash and disinfect all tools used in field dressing and extraction after use. Store game meats separately from other foods, and cook all game thoroughly according to the specific rules associated with each species.

Hunters discovering diseased animals should report this as soon as possible to game officials. In addition, hunters who go afield with hunting dogs must think of both the safety of their cherished pets and their families by making sure their dogs get the proper vaccinations for rabies and other diseases.

Appropriate Firepower

Specific laws regulate the firepower hunters must use in harvesting different types of game. Big game hunters obviously need greater

Mullaney Hardesty gets some deer-shooting pointers from her father, Mark Hardesty, at a shooting range near Detroit, Michigan.

stopping power than varmint hunters. For instance, many states ban the use of .22-caliber guns or lower for harvesting big game because they do not quickly and humanely kill larger animals. Also, while local laws might dictate the minimum power, hunters themselves may often determine stricter minimums based on their own marksmanship abilities. Shooters skilled enough to stop a deer with a lower-caliber gun can give themselves more leeway than novice shooters with the same weapon. The legal minimum is not always the wisest choice.

Young hunters, because they are often smaller and lighter in weight, may need to try out a number of firearms before they find the right one. It is unsafe for someone smaller and weaker to wield too powerful a weapon, especially when beginning his or her hunting education. Some hunters believe that too much recoil for novice shooters may encourage them to develop bad behavior—such as flinching when making a shot—or warp their instincts.

It may seem obvious, but a novice shooter should spend some initial time on a shooting range before going afield. This will build up valuable skills and confidence, and allow him or her to decide what weapon might be most comfortable and appropriate.

Far from being a mere game, a young hunter's entry into the hunting lifestyle can be a great way to learn responsibility, patience, teamwork, safety, and many other important virtues. The dangers involved in hunting and the work and preparation hunters undertake to prevent and overcome them, provide unique life lessons. Among these are core lessons of respect: for nature, animals, comrades, property, rules, and fair play. Hunting can be thrilling, and the camaraderie and fun experienced while afield is unmatched. But the wilderness is not a place for horseplay or goofing off. Taking things seriously and soberly, the beginner hunter soon learns from experience and his or her mentors that caution and intelligence should be used on the hunt.

Leaving No Trace

"Leave No Trace" is both a philosophy and the name of the organization that promotes it. It is a set of seven principles that fit in well with the hunting lifestyle: 1) Plan ahead and prepare; 2) travel and camp on durable surfaces; 3) dispose of waste properly; 4) leave what you find; 5) minimize campfire impacts; 6) respect wildlife; 7) be considerate of other visitors.

Many of these principles tie into safety, too. Someone who takes them to heart is less likely to violate important rules. Make it your business to know if and when your hunting area is under "fire season" rules, when dry and windy weather might make it dangerous to have a campfire. Keep campfires only as large as necessary to cook or provide warmth; bigger ones are a fire hazard.

Other Overnight Tips

When hunting in bear country, always bear-proof camping areas. This means minimizing smells that might attract bears. If possible, keep your cooking/kitchen area upwind of your sleeping area. Food, garbage, and anything that gives off a distinctive smell should be hung up in trees (a technique called bear bagging) at least 300 feet (91 meters) away from your camp. If camping in a treeless area, make sure to use bear-proof containers, keeping them well away from the campsite. Bears can even be attracted by items like toothpaste.

Being Thoughtful

A good hunter will avoid danger, help preserve the natural world around him or her, be thoughtful in interactions with fellow hunters

A grizzly bear rummages through a campsite. Thorough bear-proofing can prevent a rude awakening by a curious or hungry bear.

and non-hunters alike, respect wildlife, be mindful of private and public property, stay alert, and think ahead at all times. The more experience a hunter gains, the more he or she will know how all of these elements tie together. True hunters observe state and federal laws regulating game, weaponry, and tactics, and help preserve North America's wilderness through the purchase of licenses, permits, and stamps.

The information presented here is meant only as a first step into the extensive body of knowledge available on hunting safety. So much information is available online and in hunting publications and books. Experienced hunters—parents, older siblings, relatives, people in your area—also serve as invaluable mentors. Remain curious: always ask questions. Hunting safety instructors, park rangers, game officials, and many other helpful people will be happy to answer your questions, too. By asking questions, the novice hunter gains insights, some of which might even save lives when the time comes. Avoiding danger on the hunt allows you and your fellow hunters to get the most of this tradition and pass it on to others.

Happy—and safe—hunting!

backstop The terrain behind targeted game that hunters can safely shoot at without endangering themselves or others.

bear-proof To minimize smells in and around a campsite that might attract unwanted attention from bears.

bear spray A form of pepper spray developed to repel bear attacks.

diamode A medication used to treat diarrhea.

duck stamp A type of revenue stamp purchased by waterfowlers to help fund wildlife and habitat conservation.

fair chase A set of rules governing hunting tactics that aim to prevent hunters from gaining unfair advantage over game animals.

fire season A dry and windy time in the wilderness when certain activities that may cause wildfires are prohibited.

Global Positioning System (GPS) A radio navigation system that allows users to accurately determine their exact location on the earth's surface.

gunsmith A professional who fixes and otherwise services and/or modifies firearms.

harvest To kill game.

hunter orange Also known as blaze orange, a color worn by hunters to safely make their presence known to others in the field.

hydrophobic Refers to clothing materials that transfer moisture away from the wearer's skin.

hypothermia A drop in human body temperature below 95 degrees F (35 degrees C), which seriously threatens the health and life of a person.

Leave No Trace A set of seven principles adopted by hunters and other outdoors enthusiasts that seeks to minimize human impact on the wilderness.

muzzle The open end of the gun through which ammunition is discharged.

posted Refers to property that is marked with "no hunting" signs.

safety A locking device on a gun that prevents it from accidentally firing.

tree stand An elevated hunting platform affixed to a tree that gives hunters a better vantage from which to spot game.

12-20 burst A common ammunition-loading error in which a 12-gauge shell is loaded behind a 20-gauge shell, potentially causing the gun to explode.

vermin Also known regionally in some areas as "varmints," smaller animals that are often considered pests to livestock and land, such as foxes, rabbits, weasels, coyotes, and mice, among others, and sometimes hunted as game.

waders Waterproof hip boots or trousers used by waterfowlers to hunt while standing in water.

waterfowler A hunter who harvests duck, geese, or other waterfowl (game birds that swim).

Boone and Crockett Club
250 Station Drive
Missoula, MT 59801
(406) 542-1888
Web site: http://www.boone-crockett.org
The mission of the Boone and Crockett Club is to promote the conservation
    and management of wildlife (especially big game) and its habitat, to
    preserve and encourage hunting, and to maintain the highest ethical
    standards of fair chase and sportsmanship in North America.

Canadian Shooting Sports Association (CSSA)
116 Galaxy Boulevard
Etobicoke, ON M9W 5R7
Canada
(416) 679-9959
(888) 873-4339
Web site: http://www.cdnshootingsports.org
The CSSA is a Canadian organization promoting sports shooting, including
    target shooting, hunting, and archery.

Ducks Unlimited
One Waterfowl Way
Memphis, TN 38120
 (800) 45DUCKS (453-8257)
Web site: http://www.ducks.org
Ducks Unlimited, Inc., is a leading international organization that helps
    preserve wetlands, waterfowl, and the hunting tradition.

Fish and Wildlife Branch

Ministry of Forests, Lands, and Natural Resource Operations

P.O. Box 9391, STN PROV GOVT

Victoria, BC V8W 9M8

Canada

(250) 387-9771

Web site: http://www.env.gov.bc.ca/fw

The Fish and Wildlife Branch is a Canadian government agency in charge of legislation, policies, and resource management surrounding fishing and hunting activities for the nation.

International Bowhunting Organization (IBHO)

P.O. Box 398

Vermillion, OH 44089

Web site: http://www.ibo.net

The IBHO's mission is to promote bowhunting and bowhunting education worldwide.

International Hunting Education Association (IHEA)

2727 W. 92nd Avenue, Suite 103

Federal Heights, CO 80260

(303) 430-7233

Web site: http://www.ihea.com

The IHEA is a professional association promoting and overseeing hunter education throughout the United States and Canada, including seventy thousand volunteer instructors.

United States Fish & Wildlife Service (FWS)

1849 C Street Northwest

Washington, DC

(202) 208-3710

Web site: http://www.fws.gov

The U.S. Fish & Wildlife Service (FWS) is the federal government agency that helps conserve and defend fish, wildlife, plants, and their habitats.

Wildlife Conservation Society

2300 Southern Boulevard

Bronx, NY 10460

(718) 220-5100

Web site: http://www.wcs.org

The Wildlife Conservation Society has the mission to save wildlife and wild places across the globe. The organization protects many of the world's iconic creatures in the United States and abroad.

Web Sites

Due to the changing nature of Internet links, Rosen Publishing has developed an online list of Web sites related to the subject of this book. This site is updated regularly. Please use this link to access the list:

http://www.rosenlinks.com/HUNT/Hunt

FOR FURTHER READING

Carpenter, Tom. *Big Game Hunting: Bear, Deer, Elk, Sheep, and More* (Great Outdoors Sports Zone). Minneapolis, MN: Lerner Publishing Group, 2012.

Chandler, Matt. *Deer Hunting for Kids* (Edge Books: Into the Great Outdoors). Mankato, MN: Capstone Press, 2012.

DiLorenzo, Michael. *Bows, Does, & Bucks: An Introduction to Archery Deer Hunting* (Adventures with Jonny). Clinton Township, MI: Running Moose Publications, 2010.

Gross, W. H. *Young Beginner's Guide to Shooting & Archery: Tips for Gun and Bow* (The Complete Hunter). Minneapolis, MN: Creative Publishing International, 2009.

Gurtler, Janet. *Small Game* (Outdoor Hunting Guide). New York, NY: AV2/Weigl, 2012.

Hanes, Cameron R. *Backcountry Bowhunting: A Guide to the Wild Side* (Collector's Edition). Springfield, OR: CRH Publishing, 2011.

Lewis, Gary. *The Complete Guide to Hunting: Basic Techniques for Gun & Bow Hunters* (The Complete Hunter). Minneapolis, MN: Creative Publishing International, 2008.

McRae, Sloane. *Upland Hunting: Pheasant, Quail, and Other Game*. New York, NY: Rosen Publishing, 2010.

McRae, Sloane. *Waterfowl Hunting*. New York, NY: Rosen Publishing, 2010.

Peterson, Judy Monroe. *Big Game Hunting*. New York, NY: Rosen Publishing, 2011.

Petersen, Judy Monroe. *Varmint Hunting*. New York, NY: Rosen Publishing, 2011.

Shellhass, Dave, and Stephen Shellhass. *Outdoor Kids Club Ultimate Hunting Guide*. Greenville, OH: Miami Valley Outdoor Media, 2011.

Weintraub, Aileen. *Bowhunting: Revised Edition* (Great Outdoors). Mankato, MN: Capstone Press, 2007.

Wolny, Philip. *Waterfowl*. New York, NY: Rosen Publishing, 2011.

Adams, Dominic. "Injured Deer Likely Kicked, Killed Hunter." *Fort Wayne Journal Gazette*, November 16, 2011. Retrieved April 2012 (http://www. journalgazette.net/article/20111116/LOCAL07/311169959/1043/local07).

Agence France-Presse. "Dog Shoots, Kills Texas Hunter." January 8, 2008. Retrieved March 2012 (http://afp.google.com/article/ALeqM5jBqUBq3fMs rNppklpyQiHcgI6tew).

Appeal-Democrat. "Teen Accidentally Kills Cousin During Deer Hunt." Associated Press, November 29, 2011. Retrieved March 2012 (http:// www.appeal-democrat.com/articles/cousin-111811-accidentally-shot .html#ixzz1qYHevxRu).

Bourjaily, Philip. "How to Teach Your Child Gun Safety." *Field & Stream*, November 30, 2005. Retrieved March 2012 (http://www.fieldandstream. com/node/57347#).

Breaux, Jonas. "Safety Critical as Season Begins." *Advertiser*, March 24, 2012. Retrieved March 2012 (http://www.theadvertiser.com/article/ 20120325/SPORTS/203250349/Safety-critical-season-begins).

Dube, Carolyn. "Hunting Accidents a Reminder of Need for Safety." *Nashua Patch*, November 13, 2011. Retrieved March 2012 (http://nashua.patch. com/articles/hunting-accidents-a-reminder-of-need-for-safety-b36a614c).

Hurteau, Dave. "Legal, Ethical, Fair Chase: They Are Not the Same." *Field & Stream*, March 13, 2012. Retrieved March 2012 (http://www .fieldandstream.com/blogs/whitetail-365/2012/03/legal-ethical-fair- chase-they-are-not-same).

Hurteau, Dave. "When Talking Fair Chase, 'Kill' Plots and Bait Are the Same." *Field & Stream*, March 9, 2012. Retrieved March 2012 (http://www. fieldandstream.com/blogs/whitetail-365/2012/03/fair-chase-wise-bait- and-"kill"-plots-are-same).

Johnson, Akilah. "Trooper Who Shot Woman Called in Rescue." *Boston Globe*, January 4, 2012. Retrieved March 2012 (http://articles.boston

.com/2012-01-04/metro/30584449_1_james-blair-hunting-accident-
shot-woman).

Jones, J. Y. *One Man, One Rifle, One Land: Hunting All Species of Big Game in North America*. Huntington Beach, CA: Safari Press, 2001.

McCafferty, Keith. "Use Pepper Spray Instead of Guns to Stop a Charging Grizzly." *Field & Stream*, December 9, 2008. Retrieved March 2012 (http://www.fieldandstream.com/articles/hunting/2008/12/use-pepper-spray-instead-guns-stop-charging-grizzly).

McOmie, Grant. "Danger in the Wilderness." KGW.com/Newschannel 8 Portland, November 10, 2011. Retrieved April 2012 (http://www.kgw.com/lifestyle/grants-getaways/Grants-Getaways---Hurt-Hunter-in-the-Wilderness-133595143.html).

National Wild Turkey Federation. "Tree Stand Safety." Retrieved March 2012 (http://www.nwtf.org/articles.php?id=12642).

New Hampshire Fish & Wildlife. "Landowner and Hunter Frequently Asked Questions." Retrieved March 2012 (http://www.wildlife.state.nh.us/Hunting/hunt_landowner_hunter_FAQs.htm).

New York State Department of Environmental Conservation. "Hunting Safety." Retrieved March 2012 (http://www.dec.ny.gov/outdoor/9186.html).

Nickens, T. Edward. *The Total Outdoorsman Manual*. San Francisco, CA: Weldon Owen, 2011.

Painter, Doug. *The Field & Stream Firearms Safety Handbook*. Guilford, CT: The Lyons Press, 1999.

Painter, Doug. *The Hunting and Firearms Safety Primer*. Guilford, CT: Lyons Press, 1986.

Peterson, Eric. "Deer Hunting Safety." NBC 26/WGBA TV, November 17, 2011. Retrieved March 2012 (http://www.nbc26.com/news/local/134085038.html).

Pinkerton, James, and Janet Elliott. "Cheney Shooting Victim OK After Heart Attack." *Houston Chronicle*, February 15, 2006. Retrieved March 2012 (http://www.chron.com/news/houston-texas/article/Cheney-shooting-victim-OK-after-heart-attack-1896481.php).

Whelen, Townsend. *Big Game Hunting*. Whitefish, MT: Kessinger Publishing, LLC, 2008.

Zumbo, Jim. "Hunt Safe." *Outdoor Life*. Retrieved March 2012 (http://www.outdoorlife.com/node/45177#).

Zumbo, Jim. "Jim Zumbo on Hunter Safety." *Outdoor Life*, September 2007. Retrieved March 2012 (http://www.outdoorlife.com/articles/hunting/2007/09/jim-zumbo-hunter-safety).

INDEX

A

airplanes and helicopters, 43
alcohol, 6, 28
all-terrain vehicles, 43
ammunition, 21–22, 26
   importance of using appropriate, 24

B

baiting, 43–44
barrel (gun), 26
bear-proofing, 50
bear repellent, 40
bears, 37, 38, 40, 50
bison, 38
boars, 37, 38, 43
boats, 5, 33, 35
bowhunting, 9, 10, 18, 19, 28–29, 30,
   40, 44

C

camping, 15, 35, 50
Cheney, Dick, 13
clothing, 12–13, 32
compass, 35
cotton, 32

D

dangerous animals
   how to act around, 38–40
   types of, 37–38
deer, 13, 24, 43
direction, keeping a sense of, 34–35
diseases, 47
drugs, 6, 28

E

earplugs, 26
education courses for hunting, 7–10
ethics, 10, 22, 41–44

F

fair chase, 42–43, 45
fencing, as advantage in hunting, 43
firing, failure in, 24
first-aid kit, 13–15
frostbite, 31

G

gear, proper care of, 11–12
Global Positioning System (GPS), 35
guns
   care of, 26–27
   handling, 5, 6, 9–10, 27, 32, 40
   modifying, 26
   picking the appropriate firepower,
      47–49
   and safety, 17–18, 19–27, 30, 37

H

herding, as hunting method, 43
hunter orange, 12–13
hunting areas, 15–17
   getting permission, 17
   maps of, 18
   safety, 17–18
hypothermia, 6, 10, 33

L

laws, 17, 41–42, 45–47, 51
Leave No Trace, 50

About the Author

Philip Wolny is a writer, editor, and outdoors enthusiast from New York. His previous hunting-related work for Rosen Publishing includes *Waterfowl*, a beginner's introduction to the sport.

About the Consultant

Benjamin Cowan has more than twenty years of both big game and small game hunting experience. In addition to being an avid hunter, Cowan is also a member of many conservation organizations. He currently resides in west Tennessee.

Photo Credits

Cover, pp. 1, 3, 25 Comstock/Thinkstock; pp. 5, 21 Jupiterimages/Comstock/Thinkstock; pp. 8, 34, 44 © AP Images; p. 9 MCT/Getty Images; p. 11 Mike Kemp/Getty Images; p. 14 Iwona Grodzka/ Shutterstock.com; p. 16 © iStockphoto.com/Jon Huelskamp; p. 20 Paul Rackley/National Wild Turkey Federation; p. 27 Matt Lindler/National Wild Turkey Federation; p. 29 Mike Kemp Images/Stone/Getty Images; p. 31 © Alaska Stock/SuperStock; p. 33 www.johnhafnerphoto.com; p. 36 Mark Hirsch/WireImage/Getty Images; p. 39 Steve Hillebrand/USFWS; p. 42 Philippe Henry/Oxford Scientific/Getty Images; p. 46 George Gentry/USFWS; p. 48 © Jim West/The Image Works; p. 51 Mat Hayward/Shutterstock.com; cover and interior (camouflage patterns) © iStockphoto.com/molotovcoketail; back cover and interior background (landscape) Comstock/Thinkstock; back cover and interior (figure silhouettes) Hemera/Thinkstock; back cover (grass silhouette) iStockphoto.com/Makhnach_M; interior (figure silhouette) © iStockphoto.com/Michael Olson.

Designer: Nicole Russo; Photo Researcher: Marty Levick